JOURNEY THROUGH
THE UK

ANITA GANERI

W
FRANKLIN WATTS

Franklin Watts
Published in Great Britain in 2017 by The Watts Publishing Group

Credits
Editor in Chief: John Miles
Series Editor: Amy Stephenson
Series Designer: Emma DeBanks
Picture Researcher: Diana Morris

Picture Credits: Anourina/Dreamstime: 7tcb. Arenaphotouk/Dreamstime: 17b. Audines/Dreamstime: 7tl. Philiip Bird LRPS CPAGB/Shutterstock: 26. Justin Black/Dreamstime: 1, 10-11. John Braid/Dreamstime: 23b. Chris148/Dreamstime: 11t. Claffra/Shutterstock: 21 inset. Gareth Cosgrove/Dreamstime: 19t. Costasz /Dreamstime: 7cr. Paul Cowan/Dreamstime: 7bcl. Matthew Dixon/Dreamstime: 6tl., 12. Edd1979/Dreamstime: 18. Dirk Erikson/Dreamstime: 7tcrb. Michael Foley//Dreamstime: 15t. Funniefarms/Dreamstime: 7bl. Joseph Gogh/Dreamstime: 5t, 21b. Robert Harding PL/Superstock: 5b. Min Jan/Shutterstock: 7bcra. Courtesy of Jorvik Centre, York: 27t. P Kemp/Dreamstime: 13b. Shahid Khan/Dreamstime: front cover. Julius Kielaitis/Dreamstime: 4. Jan Kranendouk/Dreamstime: 25t, 25b. Anna Kucherova/Dreamstime: 3, 6bc, 24. David Lyons/Alamy: 21t. MA Photography/Shutterstock: 13t. Milosluz/Dreamstime: 7bca. Mrdoomity/Dreamstime: 7c. Roland Nagy/Dreamstime: 8c. Philkinsey/Dreamstime: 11b. Photo Library Wales/Alamy: 15b. Geoff Pickering/Dreamstime: 6br, 28. Rido/Dreamstime: 7clb. Sborisov/Dreamstime: 6tr, 9. Scenicireland.com/Christopher Hill/Alamy: 6cr, 19b. Skyscan PL/Alamy: 29c. Spumador/Shutterstock: 20. Radek Stargolewsky/Shutterstock: 27c. Stocker1970/Shutterstock: 6cl, 22-23. Petr Svec/Dreamstime: 23t. Swinnerrr/Dreamstime: 7tcl, 7bla. D J Taylor/Shutterstock: 14. Trentham/Dreamstime: 8b. Cheerapat Trinkajee/Dreamstime: 29t. Tupungato/Dreamstime: 16, 17t. Filipe Varela/Dreamstime: 7crb. Vitaly Vasin/Dreamstime: 7tc, 7tr. Dmitry Vereshchagin/Shutterstock: 7bc. wanderwolfimages/Shutterstock: 7cl. Feng Yu/Dreamstime: 7br. Yudesign/Dreamstime: 7tcr.

Dewey number: 914.1
HB ISBN: 978 1 4451 3673 8

Printed in Singapore

Franklin Watts
An imprint of
Hachette Children's Group
Part of The Watts Publishing Group
Carmelite House
50 Victoria Embankment
London EC4Y 0DZ

An Hachette UK Company
www.hachette.co.uk

www.franklinwatts.co.uk

CONTENTS

WELCOME TO THE UK!

Welcome to the UK, officially called the United Kingdom of Great Britain and Northern Ireland. Covering an area of 243,610 square kilometres, the UK lies off the north-western coast of the mainland of Europe. It has a rich history, varied culture and plenty of interesting places – both man-made and natural – to explore.

UK facts

The UK is made up of four countries – England, Scotland, Wales and Northern Ireland. Most of the territory of the UK is made up of one large island – Great Britain – which includes England, Scotland and Wales. To the west of Britain is the island of Ireland, separated by the Irish Sea. Northern Ireland occupies the north-east corner of this island. The UK has a temperate climate, but the amount of rainfall and the temperature varies depending on the season and where in the UK you are.

England has by far the largest population with around 53 million people, compared with 5 million in Scotland, 3 million in Wales and 1.8 million in Northern Ireland.

► London has the largest population of any city in the UK, with 8.6 million people.

▶ Scotland is famous for its jagged peaks and dramatic coastlines.

Your UK journey

Your journey around the UK takes you through all four countries, from the busy, crowded streets of London to the beautiful, empty beaches of the Outer Hebrides in Scotland. Along the way, you'll travel by train, plane, bus, ferry and bike – and walk through stunning scenery. You'll have the chance to visit the theatre, have a go at surfing, play the bagpipes, and maybe catch a football or rugby match.

The UK coastline

Because it is made up of one large and lots of smaller islands, the UK has a long and jagged coastline. According to Ordnance Survey, the main island of Great Britain has 17,820 km of coast. But if you add all the smaller islands, such as the Isle of Wight, the Isles of Scilly, Anglesey, and the islands off the west coast of Scotland, the total length of the UK's coastline is 31,368 km. Wherever you are in the UK, you're never further than 113 km from the sea.

Cymraeg

English is the official language and is spoken everywhere in the UK. Welsh (Cymraeg) is the other official language spoken in Wales. Road signs in Wales are in both languages, and many schools teach some or all of their lessons in Welsh. Other UK languages include Scots and Gaelic, but here are a few Welsh words for your journey.

- *Bore da* – good morning

- *Nos da* – goodnight

- *Diolch* – thank you

- *Hwyl fawr* – goodbye

◀ A street sign in both English and Welsh.

JOURNEY PLANNER

1

2

3

4

KEY

————	your route around the UK
- - - - -	flight / ferry
————	river
————	road
★	capital city

5

6

Orkney Islands

Thurso
John O'Groats

Lewis with Harris
Stornoway

St Kilda
North Uist
Isle of Skye

4

Black Cuillin

Inverness
Loch Ness

SCOTLAND

Aberdeen

South Uist
Eriskay

Fort William

Barra

Outer Hebrides

Perth

Mull

5

EDINBURGH

Berwick-upon-Tweed
Lindisfarne

Islay

Tarbert Glasgow

Melrose

Giant's
Causeway

3

Ayr

Arran

Tynemouth
Newcastle upon Tyne

**ORTHERN
ELAND**

Londonderry

Stranraer

Carlisle

Lough Neagh

*Belfast
Lough*

BELFAST

Middlesborough

Scarborough

Isle of Man
Douglas

York

Irish Sea

Blackpool

Grimsby

DUBLIN

Anglesey

*Menai
Strait*

Liverpool **Manchester**
Sheffield

**REPUBLIC
OF IRELAND**

Holyhead

Caernarfon
Porthmadog

Portmeirion

King's Lynn

Norwich

Birmingham

6

Norfolk
Broads

Cambridge

Ipswich

Aberystwyth

WALES

Stratford-upon-Avon

River Severn

St David's

Swansea

2

Oxford

River Thames

CARDIFF

Bristol

Stonehenge

LONDON

1

Salisbury

Folkestone

Dover

Brighton

Exeter

BELGIUM

Newquay

Isle of Wight

Weymouth

Plymouth

English Channel

Isles of Scilly

FRANCE

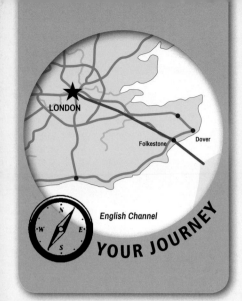

English Channel

YOUR JOURNEY

ARRIVING IN LONDON

You travel to London, the capital of England and the UK, from France on the Eurostar. This train whizzes you through the tunnel underneath the English Channel. The tunnel emerges at Folkestone on England's south coast and your train takes you through the countryside of Kent, the outskirts of London and, finally, to the city itself.

Getting around

The Eurostar arrives at St Pancras International station in central London. From here, you can take a taxi or a bus, but the city's streets are always busy and traffic can move slowly. Alternatively, head underground, to catch the 'Tube'. The London Underground system is the oldest in the world – the first line opened in 1863. It's crowded but will take you around the city quickly. The River Thames, which runs through the centre of London, provides another way of getting around and a great way to see some of the sights. Book a riverboat tour to explore the river from the Houses of Parliament to the Thames Barrier flood defences.

▲ A Eurostar train at St Pancras International.

Sporting choice

London is home to some world-famous sporting venues. If you're a sports fan, you'll be spoiled for choice. Visit Wimbledon to watch some tennis in July, Lord's or the Oval to catch a game of cricket, Wembley to see a football match, or Twickenham to experience some international rugby!

▲ Roger Federer and Novak Djokovic competing at the Wimbledon Championships.

▼ A view of the Shard, the River Thames and the London skyline.

Big business

London's economy is the biggest for any single area of the UK and the fifth biggest of any city in the world. In fact London's economy is as big as the economy of the whole of Sweden! Finance is the main business in London, but law, media, construction, manufacturing, leisure and many other industries also make a large contribution.

Why is London so successful? Excellent transport links, including rail, international airports and a large shipping port, mean easy access to other countries. Plus, English is the international language of business and the UK is located roughly halfway between North America and Asia, two major players in business around the world.

London's top five

You're spoilt for choice when it comes to sightseeing in London, but here are five highlights.

- The British Museum – London has more museums than any other city in the world and the British Museum (the world's oldest museum) has millions of objects from all over the planet.

- The Houses of Parliament – the home of the UK's government, where you can take a tour, attend a debate or marvel at the impressive clock tower that houses Big Ben.

- Shakespeare's Globe – a 1997 reconstruction of Shakespeare's original theatre built in 1599.

- The Shard – the tallest building in the EU. It has the highest viewing gallery in London at 244 m.

- The Tower of London – this fortress is over 900 years old and it contains the Crown Jewels and the Royal Mint.

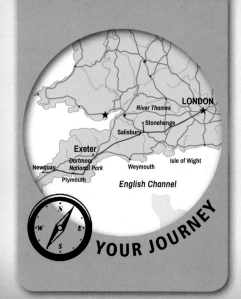

YOUR JOURNEY

LONDON TO NEWQUAY

From London, your next destination is Newquay in Cornwall, in the far south-west of England. It's a long journey, so on the way pay a visit to one of the most spectacular prehistoric monuments in the world, Stonehenge, and to Dartmoor National Park.

▶ The largest stones at Stonehenge weigh 50 tonnes.

Stonehenge

Take a train from Waterloo Station in London to Salisbury. From there, hop on the Stonehenge Tour Bus. It's a short walk from the visitor centre to the massive stone circle. The monument is more than 4,500 years old, and archaeologists think the smaller standing stones – called 'bluestones' – came from hills in South Wales, 250 km away! Experts think they were moved by rafts on rivers and hauled over the land, but no one knows for sure. The larger stones are a type of sandstone, probably from the nearby Marlborough Downs.

National parks

From Salisbury, take another coach west to Newquay. On the way you'll drive through Dartmoor, one of the UK's 15 national parks. These areas of countryside are protected by law and vary enormously in terms of terrain, from the mountains of the Cairngorms in Scotland, to the flat landscape of the Norfolk Broads (see pages 28–29). Dartmoor has a little bit of everything: rolling moors, rivers and forests and, of course, the famous Dartmoor ponies! Walking from tor to tor is a popular tourist activity here.

Surf's up!

Newquay is the surf capital of the UK, with a choice of surf schools for beginners and beautiful beaches, to suit all wind and tide conditions. The town hosts major surfing events, including the British National Championships.

▶ Surfers at Newquay's Fistral Beach.

Pasty secrets

After trying out your surfing legs you're ready for something to eat. Head to Morris Pasties in Newquay to try out a Cornish speciality. Cornish pasties have been made in Cornwall since the 14th century. Pasties were a traditional convenience food, taken to work by farm workers and tin miners. Mining was a major industry in Cornwall, but in 1988 the last mine closed. Today, tourism and dairy farming are the county's two main industries.

▶ A traditional Cornish pasty must be made in Cornwall and it must contain potato, swede, onion, beef, salt and pepper, all wrapped in pastry.

Kernowek

Alongside Scotland, Ireland, Wales, the Isle of Man and Brittany in France, Cornwall is one of the Celtic nations of Europe – where Celtic traditions, culture and language have survived. The Cornish language, Kernowek, is an important part of this heritage. It almost died out completely in the 19th century, but has been revived in recent years. In 2011, around 600 people recorded Cornish as their first language.

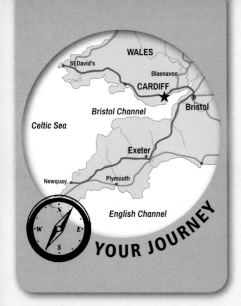

YOUR JOURNEY

NEWQUAY TO ST DAVID'S

A four-hour drive from Newquay takes you up the M5 motorway to Bristol. From here, cross the wide, muddy estuary of the River Severn, which divides England from South Wales. The motorway takes you over a high 5-km long bridge across the river. In fact, there are two Severn bridges – the older suspension bridge is a short distance upstream.

The Welsh capital

Break your journey in Cardiff, the capital of Wales. One of the best ways to see this city is by bike. Your ride takes you around Cardiff Bay, starting in front of the impressive Wales Millennium Centre, home of the Welsh National Opera. Continue past the Senedd – the main building for the National Assembly (government) of Wales and then follow the cycle path over the Cardiff Bay Barrage. This kilometre-long embankment traps water from the rivers Taff and Ely, and keeps the seawater out, to create Cardiff's beautiful freshwater bay. Then, make your way into the centre of the city, past the famous Millennium Stadium, home of Welsh rugby, to end your ride under the ancient walls of Cardiff Castle – parts of which date back to Roman times.

▼ The Senedd (right) and the Pierhead Building (left) are on the Cardiff Bay waterfront. The curved building behind them is the Wales Millennium Centre.

Coal

From Cardiff you can take a day trip north by car or train to the Big Pit Coal Museum in Blaenavon. Coal is an important fossil fuel used in the production of power around the world. Coal mining was a major industry in Wales from the time of the Industrial Revolution (see page 16), but by the 1980s the industry had declined and most mines in the UK had closed. The museum is open daily and an underground tour is a must. Find out about the history of coal, how it is extracted, the dangers of working down the pits and some tragic accidents, caused by large-scale mining in Wales.

◀ The Big Pit Coal Museum.

Smallest city

From Cardiff, a train and a bus ride take you to St David's, the smallest city in the UK, with a population of just over 1,600. By far the biggest building in this tiny city is St David's Cathedral. The cathedral you see today was begun in 1181, but it stands on the site of a much older monastery founded in the 500s CE by Dewi Sant, otherwise known as Saint David, the patron saint of Wales. His symbol – the leek – is a national symbol of Wales

Walking the coastal path

St David's lies in the county of Pembrokeshire, in the far west of South Wales. It is surrounded on three sides by sea, and many people visit the area to walk the stunning Pembrokeshire coastal path. If you can't manage all 300 km, even a short stretch is enough to show you the stunning clifftop views, wide sandy beaches, and glimpses of seals in the rocky coves below.

▼ Rugged coastlines like this form part of the Pembrokeshire Coast National Park.

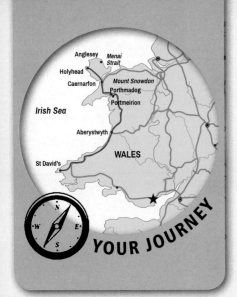

YOUR JOURNEY

ST DAVID'S TO ANGLESEY

From St David's, head north by car along the winding west coast of Wales. As you drive the views are amazing – if it's a clear day, you'll be able to see far up the coast to the mountains of Snowdonia. Before you turn off into the Snowdonia National Park, make sure you stop off at a very unusual village on the coast.

Italy in Wales

Portmeirion is entirely the work of one man – Welsh architect Sir Clough Williams-Ellis (1883–1978). He designed and built the village between 1925 and 1976, mostly in an Italian style. Williams-Ellis even saved some buildings from other parts of the country that were due to be demolished – moving them and rebuilding them, brick by brick, in Portmeirion. Today the village is a tourist resort. You can visit for a day or choose to stay in one of the buildings.

▶ Portmeirion is located on the estuary of the River Dwyryd, close to a large salt marsh. It is an important habitat for wildlife.

Snowdon's summit

Thousands of people climb Snowdon every year, taking one of the many paths to the summit. If you don't want to walk, hop on the Snowdon Mountain Railway, which opened in 1896. A welcome surprise on the summit is a café. The summit is also a unique place. It's the only place from where you can see all four countries of the UK.

▲ At 1,085 m, Mount Snowdon is the highest peak in Wales.

Exploring Snowdonia

A short distance up the road from Portmeirion is Porthmadog. Here you can hop on the narrow-gauge railway, the ideal way to explore the mountain scenery of Snowdonia as the tracks go around the foot of Mount Snowdon. The Ffestiniog Railway was originally built to transport slate from the quarries high up in the mountains to the port at Porthmadog, and the Welsh Highland Railway provided a connection through the mountains from Porthmadog to Caernarfon. Both fell into disuse after the Second World War (1939–45), but have since been restored by volunteers. Buy a train ticket for a comfortable old-fashioned carriage, pulled by a small steam train. Make sure you pack a raincoat, as Snowdonia is one of the wettest parts of both the UK and Europe!

Ynys Môn

From Caernarfon, cross the Menai Strait to the Isle of Anglesey – or Ynys Môn, in Welsh. Anglesey is the largest island in Wales, and has been inhabited since prehistoric times. If you're feeling energetic, jump on a bike and follow the route of the Tour de Môn – a popular bike race that takes you right round this beautiful island, finishing at Holyhead.

► Competitors in the Tour de Môn.

15

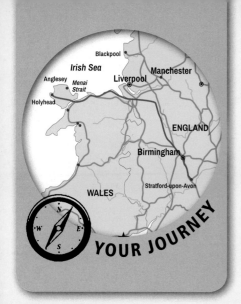

YOUR JOURNEY

ANGLESEY TO BIRMINGHAM

A fast train takes you from Holyhead back over the Menai Strait, along the coast of North Wales, and into England again. Your destination is Birmingham, the second biggest city in the UK, and a major centre of industry and commerce.

Canal trip

Birmingham was at the centre of the Industrial Revolution, with iron production, the world's first cotton mill in 1741, and large factories turning out an amazing variety of goods. All of these industries needed transport to bring coal (see page 13) and raw materials in, and to take goods out. Canals provided the answer, and by the 1820s, there was an extensive network across the city. A trip by canal boat means you can tour one of the most impressive – the New Main Line. Built by the famous Scottish engineer Thomas Telford, in the 1820s and 1830s, the New Main Line was the 'motorway' of the 19th century. Today car manufacturing and engineering continue Birmingham's industrial tradition.

The Industrial Revolution

In Britain during the 18th century, a series of inventions in manufacturing and steam power led to the start of what we now call the Industrial Revolution. This revolution meant that items, such as cloth, which had been made by hand, could now be manufactured on a much larger scale by machines driven by steam power in large factories. Developments in iron-making also allowed more iron to be produced for tools, machines and structures, such as bridges.

◀ Today, the canals are mainly used for leisure; transporting people instead of goods.

▶ The bronze sculpture of a bull at the Bull Ring represents the city's power and strength.

Old and new

Your canal tour takes you past some very modern landmarks, including the National Indoor Arena, a huge entertainment centre that hosts everything from athletics to concerts by world famous music stars. Once you're safely back on dry land, don't forget to check out the vast shopping centre at the Bull Ring. Located in the heart of the city, the Bull Ring has been a commercial centre since a market was first held here in 1154 during the Middle Ages.

Shakespeare's birthplace

It's a short drive out of Birmingham to the historic town of Stratford-upon-Avon. Tourists visit the town from all over the world because this is where the playwright William Shakespeare was born. Pay a visit to Shakespeare's birthplace on Henley Street, and his grave in Holy Trinity Church. You could also go to a performance of one of his plays at the Swan Theatre or the Royal Shakespeare Theatre, which are both situated on the north bank of the River Avon.

▲ This statue of Shakespeare can be visited in Bankcroft Gardens, Stratford-upon-Avon.

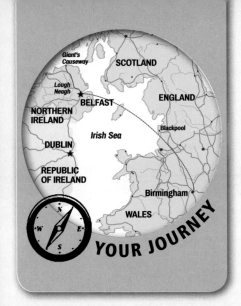

YOUR JOURNEY

BIRMINGHAM TO BELFAST

It's a short flight from Birmingham International Airport to Belfast, the capital of Northern Ireland. As you fly into Belfast, look out for the waters of Lough Neagh, the largest freshwater lake in the UK, stretching beneath you.

About Northern Ireland

Northern Ireland covers about one-sixth of the island of Ireland, and it shares a land border with the Republic of Ireland, which is a separate country. Northern Ireland came into being in 1921, when Ireland was split in two. Many people in Northern Ireland – mostly Protestants – wanted to remain part of the UK (Nationalists). A minority – mostly Catholics – wanted to be part of an independent, united Ireland (Unionists). Violence often known as 'the Troubles', between the Nationalists and Unionists started in the late 1960s, and continued until the Good Friday Agreement of 1998.

▲ The 106-m tall *Samson* is the crane in the background; *Goliath*, in the foreground, is 96 m tall.

Samson and Goliath

Belfast lies at the mouth of the River Lagan, where it empties into Belfast Lough, an inlet of the Irish Sea, making it an ideal location for shipbuilding. In the early 18th century, the city's main shipbuilder, Harland and Wolff, was one of the biggest in the world, employing thousands of people in the city. Look for *Samson* and *Goliath* on the city's skyline – two huge cranes used for building and repairing ships today. The most famous ship built in these docks was also the unluckiest – the RMS *Titanic* hit an iceberg on its maiden voyage and sank.

Tourist attractions

During the Troubles, Belfast suffered terrible violence and frequent bomb attacks. But since the end of the conflict, the city has flourished. With attractions such as the Waterfront Hall – a concert and conference centre – and the Titanic Belfast building, thousands of tourists now come to Belfast every year. Golf is a popular activity here, and Belfast has 14 courses for visitors to choose from. Belfast is also home to Northern Ireland's government building, Stormont, where the Northern Ireland Assembly meets.

▲ The Stormont Parliament Building.

Giant's Causeway

A bus tour out of the city will take you to one of the wonders of the world – the Giant's Causeway. This amazing site, on the north coast of Northern Ireland, is the result of an ancient volcanic eruption. You can walk on the columns of lava, called basalt, which extend from the clifftop into the sea. There are about 40,000 of them.

▼ Most of the rock columns that make up the Giant's Causeway are hexagonal in shape.

19

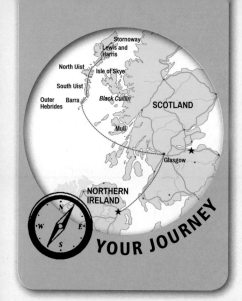

YOUR JOURNEY

BELFAST TO ISLE OF HARRIS

Your next stop is the islands of the Outer Hebrides off the west coast of Scotland. The quickest way to get there is by plane. Fly from Belfast to Scotland's largest city – Glasgow. There, board a small aircraft that takes you west to a very exciting destination!

A bumpy landing

▲ Only small planes are able to land on the wide, flat, white sands of Barra airport.

The airport on Barra, at the southern end of the Outer Hebrides, is situated next to the beach – and the landing strip is the beach. Flights are timed to coincide with low tide, as at high tide the runway is underwater. It's quite an experience to land here – the wind blows the small, 20-seater plane around as it touches down! But looking out of the window, you can see why this airport has been voted the most scenic in the world – and its landing strip the most treacherous.

Beautiful islands

It's a short hop on the bus to catch a ferry across the Sound of Barra to the next island, Eriskay. From there, travel northwards across a causeway that links Eriskay to South Uist (see below) and on through North Uist. Another short journey on a ferry takes you to South Harris. Everywhere you look, the scenery is spectacular – white sandy beaches, rocky outcrops, and grassy areas covered in wild flowers known as 'machair'.

Ancient rocks

You reach the port of Tarbert on South Harris, which has a population of around 550 people. Tarbert may be small, but it is an important transport hub for the islands. From there, you can see the rugged mountains of North Harris. Most of the rocks that make up the islands of the Outer Hebrides are Lewisian gneiss – named after the Isle of Lewis, which lies to the north of Harris. They are the oldest rocks in the UK, dating back 3,000 million years.

Harris Tweed

For centuries, the islanders of the Outer Hebrides have woven a cloth called tweed in their homes. The tweed is made from sheep's wool, coloured with natural dyes before it is woven into lengths of cloth. Only wool from the Cheviot and Scottish Blackface sheep are used. This traditional product is still woven on the islands, and is sold all over the world.

▲ A traditional Harris Tweed weaver with his cloth.

St Kilda

Around 70 km west of Harris lies St Kilda, 'the islands at the edge of the world'. People lived on these remote islands until 1930, when the harsh conditions, many cases of pneumonia and lack of regular contact with the mainland forced the small community to leave. The entire population moved to mainland Scotland. Today, St Kilda is a World Heritage Site, and an important breeding place for seabirds.

▲ These stone huts (*cleits*) are only found on the islands of St Kilda.

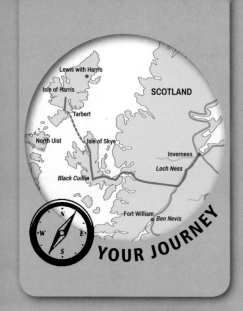

YOUR JOURNEY

HARRIS TO INVERNESS

Another ferry from Tarbert takes you south-east to the Isle of Skye, the largest island of the Inner Hebrides. Skye is famous for its spectacular mountain scenery. As you drive south across the island, you can see the soaring peaks and sharp ridges of the Black Cuillin.

▼ There are 12 peaks over 900 m high in the Black Cuillin mountain range.

The Inaccessible Pinnacle

The Black Cuillin mountain range has some of the most challenging walking and climbing routes in the UK. Its rocky peaks rise straight out of the sea, and are the remains of an ancient volcano. Put on your walking boots and head up a path that takes you into Coire Lagan – a bowl-shaped valley with a small loch (lake), surrounded by towering mountain peaks. From here, you can see the Inaccessible Pinnacle – the most difficult-to-reach mountain summit in the UK.

Loch Ness Monster

Say goodbye to Skye as you drive across the Skye Bridge to the mainland. Your route takes you east through the Scottish Highlands to Loch Ness. This huge freshwater lake is one of the deepest in Scotland – 230 m at its deepest point. It contains more water than all the lakes of England and Wales put together. According to legend, it has a mysterious monster, known as Nessie. Take a cruise on the *Nessie Hunter* and see if you can catch sight of the famous creature. Around 400,000 tourists visit the area each year and she has not been spotted yet!

Caledonian Canal

Continue your journey on a different boat along the Caledonian Canal to Inverness. The canal was designed by Thomas Telford and took 19 years to build. It follows a natural fault line called the Great Glen Fault and it connects Inverness in the north with Fort William to the south, a distance of 97 km. Only one-third of this is man-made, the rest of the route being lochs, one of which is Loch Ness.

Your trip takes you through several locks and through the dramatic scenery of the Highlands. Sadly you won't catch a glimpse of Ben Nevis, the UK's highest mountain. This 1,344 m peak is located in the southern end of the Highlands, close to Fort William.

▲ A Caledonian Canal lock at Fort Augustus on Loch Ness.

Bagpipes

The Great Highland bagpipes are Scotland's national instrument. The bagpipes are played as a solo instrument, or together in pipe bands. Have a go at playing one. It takes a lot of puff and is a lot harder than it looks!

▶ A pipe band play at a Highland Games event.

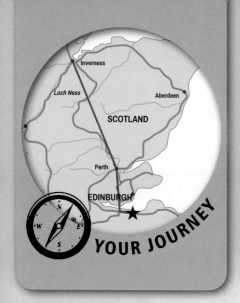

INVERNESS TO EDINBURGH

From Inverness, take the train south to Scotland's capital city, Edinburgh, in the Lowlands. As you near Edinburgh, the train crosses one of the best-known landmarks in Scotland – the spectacular Forth Bridge.

The Forth Bridge

Before the bridge was built, the only way to transport goods across the estuary was by ferry. This crossing was so busy it became clear that an alternative was needed. When it opened in 1890, the Forth Bridge was the largest structure in the UK to be made from steel. Its cantilever design was groundbreaking, and has withstood the test of time, as the bridge has been carrying trains for over 100 years. But the pioneering design of another Scottish railway bridge, over the River Tay, was not so successful. Tragically, it collapsed during a storm in 1879, killing 75 people.

▲ The Forth Bridge spans the Firth of Forth, a major estuary on the east coast of Scotland.

▲ Actors perform their show in the streets at the Edinburgh Fringe.

Celebrations

Two of Edinburgh's most famous events are its festival and its New Year celebrations. The Edinburgh International Festival takes place every summer, and draws performers and audiences from all over the world. The main festival includes theatre and opera productions, concerts, dance and a literary festival. Alongside this is the Fringe – an arts festival that includes everything from children's shows to comedy. At New Year, or 'Hogmanay', Edinburgh also puts on a great show, with firework displays, pipe bands, processions and street parties.

Edinburgh Castle

You arrive in the centre of Edinburgh and set off to explore the city on foot. Your first stop is Edinburgh's magnificent castle (see below, right), perched on a rocky outcrop overlooking the city. The oldest part of the castle, St Margaret's Chapel, dates back to the 12th century. You can see the Scottish Crown Jewels here, and the Stone of Scone – a block of sandstone on which all Scottish monarchs were crowned, until it was stolen by Edward I of England in 1296. Look out for Mons Meg, a huge medieval cannon that dates from 1449.

Scottish Parliament

From the castle, take a walk down the Royal Mile, so-called because Holyrood Palace is at its far end. Your destination, however, is the Scottish Parliament Building, which was opened in 2004. Scotland has had its own government, separate from the United Kingdom Parliament, since 1999. In 2014, Scottish citizens voted in an historic referendum, which if a majority 'yes' vote had won, would have meant that Scotland would no longer be a part of the UK. As Scotland voted 'no' it remains a country of the UK.

Edinburgh economy

Edinburgh is one of the most powerful and successful cities in the UK. Like London, if you can think of an industry then it is represented here. Finance and technology feature heavily, as does education. Edinburgh University is consistently ranked in the top 20 in the world and has a leading medical school.

▲ Edinburgh Castle sits on Castle Rock, which is a huge lump of volcanic rock.

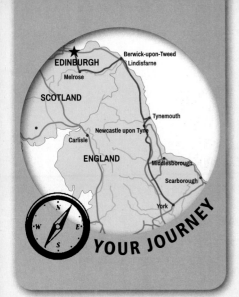

YOUR JOURNEY

EDINBURGH TO YORK

For the next stage of your journey, cycle from Edinburgh to Tynemouth along Route 1 of the National Cycle Network (NCN) – a series of quiet roads and paths that cover the whole of the UK.

Through the Borders

Route 1 is 2,728 km long, running from Dover in the south-east of England to the Shetland Islands in the far north of Scotland, but you're only tackling a small section. First, head south out of Edinburgh into a region known as the Scottish Borders. From the pretty town of Melrose, follow the River Tweed to the coast, crossing the Scotland-England border to reach Berwick-upon-Tweed, the northernmost town in England. Your route now winds south along the beautiful coastline of Northumberland.

Lindisfarne

Route 1 takes you to Lindisfarne (also called Holy Island), 1.6 km off the Northumbrian coast. At low tide, a causeway connects the island and the mainland, so you can cycle across. But be careful – it's dangerous to try to cross when the tide is sweeping in. A monastery was founded on Lindisfarne in the 600s CE by an Irish monk called Aidan (c. 590–651 CE). Take a tour of the island to see the now ruined monastery, the castle and the lime kilns. Lime was once a major part of the economy of this tiny island.

Early Christianity in Britain

Christianity first came to Britain in around 200 CE with the Romans. When the Romans left, Christianity survived mainly on the western edges of Britain – in Wales and Ireland. This is why Aidan came over from Ireland, to try to spread the Christian faith in the north of England.

▲ The Castle on Lindisfarne was built in 1550 to defend against attack from Scotland.

Historic York

End your cycle ride in Tynemouth and jump on a train to York, the county town of Yorkshire and a favourite destination for tourists. York was founded by the Romans in 71 CE, captured and expanded by the Vikings in the 9th century CE, and taken over by William the Conqueror in 1068. Work started on the cathedral (York Minster) in 1080. Climb the steps to the top of the central tower to be rewarded with stunning views across the city.

▼ York Minster dominates the skyline of York.

Jorvik

To find out more about Viking York – Jorvik – visit the Jorvik Viking Centre. It stands on the site of a massive archaeological dig that uncovered the houses, shops and workplaces of Jorvik beneath the modern-day streets of York. It recreates life 1,000 years ago – all the sights and sounds. You even smell some Viking cooking and an authentic Viking cesspit!

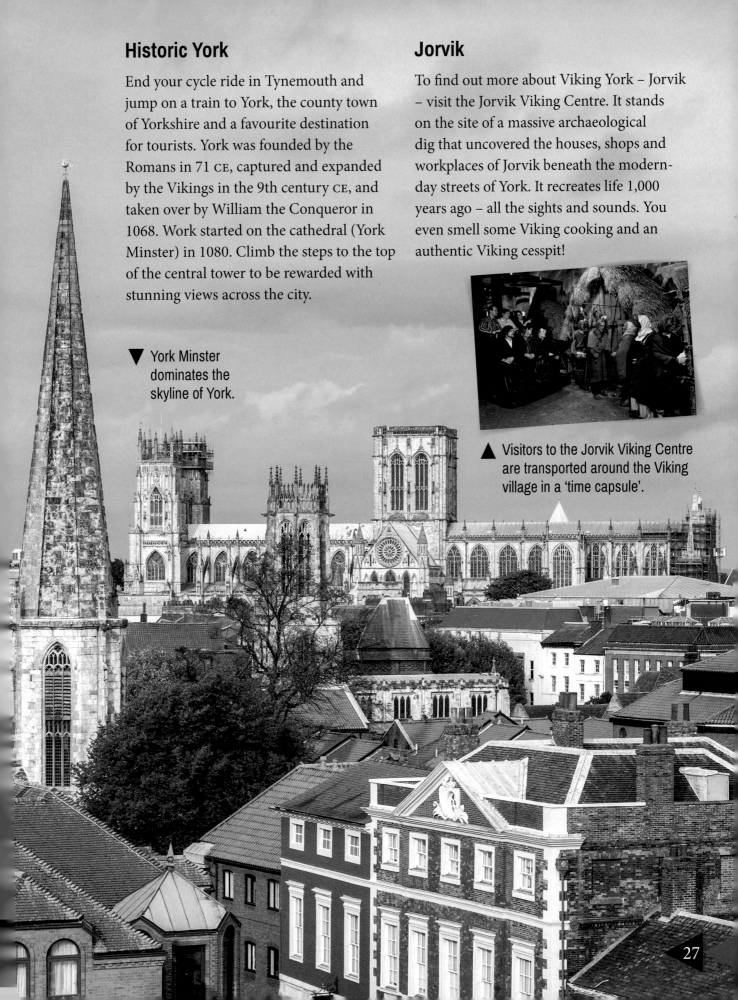

▲ Visitors to the Jorvik Viking Centre are transported around the Viking village in a 'time capsule'.

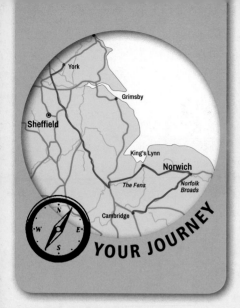

YOUR JOURNEY

YORK TO CAMBRIDGE

From York, drive south on the A1 – a major road that connects Edinburgh and London. Your destination is Cambridge in East Anglia. But first, you take a diversion to find out about a very special area of wetlands – known as the Norfolk Broads.

The Broads

This region of waterways and marshes covers 300 square km across the counties of both Norfolk and Suffolk. The best way to see the Broads is by boat. If you're lucky you can catch a ride on one of the few remaining traditional sailing barges, known as wherries. Wherry Albion (see right) has a huge black sail, and is 18 m long. In the 19th century, hundreds of wherries transported goods up and down these waterways. Today, there are just eight left on the Broads.

▶ The Broads is ideal for sailing as it is often windy. This is due to its flat landscape and location close to the coast.

Natural or man-made?

Until the 1960s, people thought that the waterways of the Norfolk Broads were entirely natural. Then, new research showed that humans had created the Broads. In medieval times, people dug peat for fuel, creating large pits that gradually began to fill with water. So the landscape we see today was partly man-made.

▶ Punters on the River Cam near Clare College Bridge – the oldest bridge in Cambridge.

▼ One of the more unusual Norfolk crops – tulips!

The Fens

From the Broads, drive to King's Lynn and then south through huge flat fields, covered by crops, and divided by deep drainage channels. This area, known as the Fens, was once boggy marshland that regularly flooded. From the 17th century onwards, people built channels to drain the land to make fields. Farming is still one of the main industries in this part of the UK. In the past, windmills powered pumps to remove water from the fields. Today, the Fens are protected from floods by high embankments, and nearly 300 pumping stations.

Cambridge

Across the flat fields, you'll see the buildings of Cambridge on the skyline long before you reach the city. Cambridge is famous worldwide for its university, founded in 1209, and is a popular tourist destination. The city centre is full of bikes – it's the best way to get around the busy streets. See the sights from the River Cam, which runs through the middle of the city.

Punting

End your UK journey by hopping into a punt – a flat-bottomed boat, propelled along with a long pole. The River Cam is shallow, making it ideal for punting. Your route takes you along the 'Backs', from where you can see the magnificent buildings of several Cambridge colleges including St John's, Clare and King's. Punting may be old-fashioned, but Cambridge is a city at the forefront of modern medicine, technology, research and development.

GLOSSARY

archaeologist
A person who studies the past by looking at the remains of buildings, tools and other items that people long ago have left behind.

architect
A person who designs buildings and supervises their construction.

Backs
The backs of some of the colleges in Cambridge, along the River Cam.

basalt
A dark-coloured volcanic rock.

cantilever bridge
A bridge in which each span is a cantilever, supported at one end only.

causeway
A raised path or road which crosses water or marshland.

cesspit
A pit where rubbish was thrown into and which also doubled up as a toilet.

Crown Jewels
The collection of crowns, rings, orbs, swords and other objects used for royal ceremonies, such as the coronation of a king or queen.

embankments
Banks of earth or stone that are built to hold water back.

estuary
The wide channel of a river where it flows into the sea.

EU
Short for the European Union, a group of European countries that work together.

fossil fuel
Any fuel that occurs naturally, such as coal, oil or natural gas.

Good Friday Agreement
A major political agreement, which was signed on Good Friday on 10 April 1998, between the British and Irish governments, and all the political parties of Northern Ireland. They agreed that Northern Ireland would remain a part of the UK until the majority of the people of Northern Ireland decided they wanted to be part of a united Ireland instead. The Good Friday Agreement was part of a wider peace process that helped bring to an end the Troubles in Northern Ireland.

Highland Games
Events held in the spring and summer that celebrate Scottish and Gaelic culture. Games events include the caber (large pine log) toss, the Scottish hammer throw and competitions in piping (bagpipes) and drumming.

lime
A white powder produced by heating limestone. Lime is used to make other materials, such as concrete and fertiliser.

lock
A man-made chamber on a river or canal that is used to raise or lower boats between different water levels.

machair
A piece of sandy, grassy land above the shore, found in the north of Scotland.

narrow gauge
A railway with a smaller distance between the lines than a standard gauge.

Nationalists
People in Northern Ireland who wish to remain part of the UK.

Ordnance Survey
The official map-making body of the British government.

patron saint
A saint who is particularly associated with something. This association can range from a nation, place or job to a craft or activity.

peat
A brown material made of partly-rotted plant matter. It can be dried and used as a gardening material or burnt as fuel.

prehistoric
From a time long ago, before writing was invented.

punt
A flat-bottomed wooden boat, propelled along a river by a punter with a long pole.

referendum
When people vote on a matter of public importance. Usually (but not always) a vote of 'yes' or 'no' on a single matter.

Royal Mint
The only company legally allowed to make the coins of the United Kingdom.

salt marsh
Land that is regularly flooded by the tides, but that supports plant and animal life. Trees and other plants that grow on salt marshes are adapted to live in an area with high levels of salt in the soil.

sandstone
A type of rock made from tiny fragments of quartz, feldspar and other minerals. It can be pink or yellow in colour and is used in buildings.

temperate
Having a mild climate that is between polar and tropical.

terrain
A piece of ground and its characteristics, such as being rocky.

tor
A high, rocky hill.

Unionists
People in Northern Ireland who wish to be part of a united Ireland.

wetlands
An area of marshy land which provides a rich habitat for plants and animals.

wherries
Traditional wooden sailing barges, used in Norfolk, England.

BOOKS TO READ

The Rough Guide to Great Britain by Jules Brown (Rough Guide, 2015)

Lonely Planet Great Britain by Neil Wilson (Lonely Planet, 2015)

Lonely Planet Discover Great Britain by Neil Wilson (Lonely Planet, 2015)

Lonely Planet Ireland by Fionn Davenport (Lonely Planet, 2014)

DK Eyewitness Travel Guide: Great Britain by Michael Leapman (Dorling Kindersley, 2014)

The Real: UK by Paul Mason (Franklin Watts, 2015)

Not For Parents London by Klay Lamprell (Lonely Planet, 2011)

Seashore Safaris: Exploring the Seashores of the United Kingdom by Judith Oakley (Graffeg, 2011)

WEBSITES

http://www.roughguides.com/country/england/
http://www.roughguides.com/country/wales/
http://www.roughguides.com/country/scotland/
http://www.roughguides.com/country/ireland/

These Rough Guide websites are packed with interesting and useful information for your visit to the United Kingdom. There are tips on where and when to travel, including lots of great itineraries to inspire your own journey around the UK.

http://www.lonelyplanet.com/great-britain
http://www.lonelyplanet.com/ireland

Lonely Planet's websites are a great introduction to the UK and tell you about the best places to visit, historical and geographical information, food and drink to sample, and practical hints and tips about money, health, languages and local customs.

http://www.visitbritain.com/en/EN/

A brilliant site with lots of places to visit, things to do, tips about accommodation and transport, and lots more about Britain.

Note to parents and teachers:
Every effort has been made by the Publishers to ensure that the websites in this book are suitable for children, that they are of the highest educational value, and that they contain no inappropriate or offensive material. However, because of the nature of the Internet, it is impossible to guarantee that the contents of these sites will not be altered. We strongly advise that Internet access is supervised by a responsible adult.

INDEX